No Rules–No Ruler

Appliqué
Outside
the **Lines**

with Piece O' Cake Designs

Becky Goldsmith & Linda Jenkins

C&T PUBLISHING

Text and artwork copyright © 2009 by Becky Goldsmith and Linda Jenkins

Artwork copyright © 2009 by C&T Publishing, Inc.

PUBLISHER: Amy Marson

CREATIVE DIRECTOR: Gailen Runge

EDITORS: Lynn Koolish and Kesel Wilson

TECHNICAL EDITORS: Carol Zentgraf and Mary Flynn

COPYEDITOR/PROOFREADER: Wordfirm Inc.

COVER/BOOK DESIGNER: Kristy K. Zacharias

PAGE LAYOUT ARTIST: Kerry Graham

PRODUCTION COORDINATOR: Casey Dukes

ILLUSTRATOR: Becky Goldsmith

PHOTOGRAPHY by Christina Carty-Francis and Diane Pedersen of C&T Publishing, Inc., unless otherwise noted.

Published by C&T Publishing, Inc., P.O. Box 1456, Lafayette, CA 94549

Library of Congress Cataloging-in-Publication Data

Goldsmith, Becky

Appliqué outside the lines with Piece O' Cake Designs : no rules-no ruler / Becky Goldsmith and Linda Jenkins.

    p. cm.

Includes index.

Summary: "Break the rules by using new improvisational techniques for 8 appliqué projects from Piece O' Cake Designs. Learn to let go and be more improvisational in how you piece, cut, and place designs"—Provided by publisher.

ISBN 978-1-57120-609-1 (paper trade : alk. paper)

1. Machine appliqué—Patterns. 2. Machine quilting—Patterns. I. Jenkins, Linda II. Piece O' Cake Designs. III. Title.

TT779.G62942 2009

746.44'5041—dc22

                              2008045253

Printed in China

10 9 8 7 6 5 4 3

Contents

Acknowledgments

No one stands alone, and we are no exception. Many people helped us with this book. Lynn Koolish, our editor, has worked with us for many years, and we value her commitment to excellence and attention to detail. She has once again refined our manuscript into a very readable book.

The photos are lovely to look at, and we have the C&T photography studio to thank for that. The eye-catching cover and cheerful and easy-to-navigate book design are the product of Kristy Zacharias's time and effort. Carol Zentgraf made sure that the illustrations were correct and easy to use (and we know how important that is to you, readers!). Casey Dukes, the production coordinator, kept everything running smoothly. These and so many more talented people make us look good!

Last, but certainly not least, we thank Todd Hensley, CEO, and Amy Marson, publisher, of C&T. They made a commitment to us many years ago and have never let us down. We appreciate all that you have done and continue to do for us.

Dedication

From Becky . . .

My sister, Christy Eckroat, has polycystic kidney disease. There is no cure for PKD, and no one knows what causes it. Christy is two years younger than I am. Like many sisters, we have been both close and not so close over the years. I'm happy to say that lately we have been closer than ever.

As the disease has progressed, I have been amazed at the way Christy faces each day. She is in a lot of pain—more than I think I could cope with. However, she is strong-willed (stubborn) enough to refuse to give in to it!

Christy doesn't complain—about the pain or the total unfairness of it all. She has not let her illness define who she is. My sister has made a conscious choice to *live* every day to its fullest. She is an inspiration to me—and a reminder to make the time to enjoy those I love.

Christy and Becky (Photo by Elizabeth Eckroat.)

Introduction

We think of quilts as explosions of color, but quilts are also about lines. Where one fabric stops and another begins, a line is drawn. An artist can make a line more interesting by varying its weight and density. For example, a pencil line on rough paper is much different from one drawn on smooth paper. A painter can make a line sharp or feathered. However, it's hard to do any of this with a seamline.

In 2005, Ami Simms invited me to submit a quilt to the Alzheimer's Art Quilt Initiative. (For more on this wonderful project, go to www.AlzQuilts.org.) I gave a great deal of thought to the kind of image I would use in my quilt and decided that I would approach the quilt as if I had Alzheimer's. I knew that if diagnosed I would still quilt, but that over time my sewing abilities would diminish.

I designed a traditional appliqué block for the quilt. I made the center block as perfect as I could make it. As I moved away from the center, however, the shapes, colors, and stitching became much less precise. I didn't use a pattern for the border. Instead, I randomly pulled scrap fabric from a pile and haphazardly cut stems and leaves. I used heavy black thread for the border appliqué. I believe this is one of the most interesting quilts I have ever made.

In making this quilt, I realized that I am so used to following my pattern that *not doing so* was hard. But the more I sewed, the more I found myself enjoying the freedom of not following the lines. It was not about being sloppy; it was about making more interesting lines in the quilt!

Since finishing *Trying to Hold On*, I became very interested in playing with the lines in my quilts. I put away my ruler and cut freely with my rotary cutter. I measured by eye. You'd think this would have made things faster, but for me it did not. It did, however, engage a different part of my quiltmaking brain, and that was both fun and invigorating.

Artists are very aware of negative space. It is defined as the empty and seemingly unimportant background space in a two- or three-dimensional artwork. In fact, the negative space surrounds and supports the positive space. You can't have one without the other. The quilting equivalent of negative space is the background fabric. Linda and I

Trying to Hold On made by Becky Goldsmith, 2005. Photo by Lee A. F. Kirchner

are known for piecing together different fabrics—prints, plaids, stripes, and solids in all manner of colors—to use behind our appliqué. We have always preferred a more active negative space.

The quilts in this book push that idea a little further. The negative space is more heavily pieced and asymmetrical. The seamlines are organic—they are not ruler straight. The outer edges of most of the quilts are cut by hand. These quilts are not truly square. The organic outer edges enhance the lines in the quilt rather than boxing them in.

This book is about the *process* of working in a freer and more organic manner—stepping away from the sharp lines and measurements that come with rulers, and feeling free to alter the appliqué pattern if it suits you. However, we all know that there is no one perfect way to make a quilt. For that reason, the instructions for the quilts in this book are written so that you can work with straight lines and a ruler if you prefer. In either case, it is our hope that you enjoy thinking about the design of your quilts in a new way.

– Becky Goldsmith

Basic Supplies

Fabric The most common quilting fabric is 100% cotton. It is readily available, affordable, and easy to sew. *Always prewash your cotton fabric.*

Rotary cutter and mat For most cutting, including cutting strips, trimming blocks to size, and cutting borders, rotary cutting tools give the best results. *A rotary ruler is optional for these quilts.*

Fabric scissors Small, sharp scissors are best for clipping threads and trimming fabric. Shears are best for cutting long edges.

Paper scissors Small, sharp scissors are more precise than long shears for cutting templates.

Clear vinyl To make the positioning overlay, use 18"-wide Quilter's Vinyl or 54"-wide clear, medium-weight upholstery vinyl from a store that carries upholstery fabric. Save any tissue paper that comes with the vinyl.

Permanent markers To mark the positioning overlay, a black Sharpie Ultra Fine Point Permanent Marker works best.

Pencils We use either a General's Charcoal white pencil, a General's Sketch & Wash, or a mechanical Ultimate Marking Pencil for quilters to mark fabric when necessary.

Sewing machine For *piecing*, you need a sewing machine in good working order that sews a straight stitch. Successful *machine quilting* requires the best sewing machine that you can afford. In both cases, it's really helpful to have a table that your machine fits into.

We love our Berninas! The Berninas with a stitch regulator are particularly suited for free-motion quilting.

Wooden toothpick Use a round, wooden toothpick to help turn under the turn-under allowance at points and curves. Wood has a texture that grabs and holds the fabric.

Batting We prefer to use Fairfield's bamboo/cotton or a 100% cotton (or a cotton/bamboo blend) batting.

Thread Use cotton thread with cotton fabric.

Appliqué thread There are many brands to choose from. Work with different brands until you find the ones that work best for you. We prefer a finer cotton thread, such as Superior's MasterPiece, Aurifil 50-weight thread, Mettler 60-weight machine embroidery thread, DMC 50-weight machine embroidery thread, or YLI Soft Touch thread.

 tip We have worked with Superior Threads to put together sets of MasterPiece thread called Frostings. The thread is prewound onto bobbins especially for appliquérs. The 36 different colors come in 3 sets of 12. Each bobbin holds 85 yards of thread. Small, compact, and convenient, these bobbin sets are a great way to carry your thread.

Piecing thread All-purpose cotton threads, such as those made by Gütermann and Mettler, work well for piecing. If you prefer a finer cotton thread, use one of our appliqué thread choices. When piecing with a finer thread, shorten your stitch length.

Machine quilting thread When we want the thread to be less obvious, we use the finer threads listed above for our machine quilting. When we want a higher-profile thread, we use King Tut by Superior Threads. Because we quilt heavily, the finer thread works well. If you plan to quilt farther apart, however, you should use a heavier thread.

Hand quilting thread We like Gütermann's hand quilting thread.

Needles Use the appropriate needle for the job at hand.

Hand appliqué needles For hand appliqué, we use a size 11 Hemming & Son milliner's needle. If you prefer a shorter needle, Clover's Gold Eye size 12 is nice. There are many good needles; find the one that fits *your* hand.

Sewing machine needles For piecing and quilting, use sharps needles rather than universal needles. We usually use an 80/12 (medium size) or a 70/10 (finer size) needle, depending on the fabric and thread we are using.

Pins We use pins when doing appliqué and piecing.

Appliqué pins Use ½″ sequin pins to pin the appliqué pieces in place. Use larger flower-head quilting pins to hold the positioning overlay in place where necessary.

Piecing pins Use long, fine pins for piecing. We like very fine glass-head pins (0.5mm) or Clover's flower-head pins.

Clear, heavyweight, self-laminating sheets Use these sheets to make templates. You can find them at most office supply stores, online, and sometimes at warehouse markets. Buy the single-sided sheets, not the pouches. If you can't find the laminate, use clear Contac paper—it'll work in a pinch (refer to Making the Appliqué Templates on pages 52–53).

Sandpaper board When tracing templates onto fabric, place the fabric on the sandpaper side of the board. Sandpaper boards are available in quilt shops, or you can make your own by gluing very-fine-grit sandpaper to a thin piece of fiberboard (such as Masonite), plywood, or foam-core board.

Fusible web If you prefer to fuse and machine stitch the appliqué, use a paper-backed fusible web. Choose the one you like best, and follow the manufacturer's directions. It's a good idea to test the fusible web on the fabric that you will be using.

Nonstick pressing sheet If you are doing fusible appliqué, a non-stick pressing sheet will protect the iron and ironing board.

A good light Sewing is so much easier when you can see what you are doing. A floor lamp is particularly nice, as you can position it over your shoulder.

Quilting gloves Gloves make it easier to hold onto the quilt during machine quilting. We like the Machingers brand.

Color and Contrast

Color is the first thing you see when you look at a quilt. Color will draw you into a quilt or push you away. It is a delight to work with colors you like, and a chore to work with colors you don't. It seems obvious—work with colors you like, and be happy. However, as you spend time making more quilts, you will find that the color palette that makes you happy is expanding. Colors you didn't like much before will likely start to look better and better. Try to keep an open mind when working with color.

Contrast and Value

As important as color is to a quilt, the contrast between values is at least as important. Every color has a *value*—is the color light, medium, or dark? *Contrast* is the difference between two or more values. The contrast between different values is what makes a design visible. High-contrast fabrics placed next to each other are very visible, while fabrics low in contrast next to each other run together.

Look at the grayscale. As the squares get darker, the black numbers become harder to see. In #8, there is no contrast between the black number and the box—the number is there, but you can't see it.

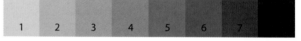

As boxes get darker, numbers are harder to see.

There is a lot of contrast between light and dark values, as you can see when we place boxes #1 and #8 next to each other. They are *high* in contrast; it's easy to tell them apart from a distance.

High contrast is easy to see.

It is more difficult to see the difference between values that are similar to each other, because they are *low* in contrast. It can be hard to tell them apart at any distance.

Low contrast is harder to see.

Placing high-contrast fabrics next to each other in your quilt is one sure way to make that part of the design stand out. If you want to subdue an area, use fabrics of lower contrast. Most successful quilts have areas of both high and low contrast.

Be aware that just because two fabrics are different colors does not mean that the fabrics are different values. The blue and green in the photo are different colors, but they look nearly the same. If you use them next to each other in a quilt, you may not be able to distinguish blue pieces from green pieces, and that could ruin your design.

Different colors can look similar when their values are similar.

It is also true that value is relative. A light yellow can be very visible against a dark yellow. But the darkest yellow would still look very light against black. Always group together the fabrics that you plan to use in a particular quilt to evaluate which are light, medium, or dark.

Designs on Fabric

Fabric comes in solid colors—and everything else.

Solid colors are just that—solid color. It's easy to think of solids as boring, but that's not true. Amish quilts, which are usually made only with solid fabrics, are wonderfully graphic. Many of today's art quilters use solids, much as a painter would use paint, to create amazing quilts.

The "everything else" category is pretty crowded. A printed fabric can have any design imaginable on it: tiny little bugs, huge flowers, dinosaurs, dots, stripes—anything. Some prints are so subtle they almost look like solids. Others, composed of colors high in contrast, are very active.

Woven designs are most often stripes and plaids. Different colors of thread are woven together to create a pattern. Where the different colors of thread cross, they blend to create a new color. Woven fabrics are great bridges from one color to another because of these blended areas. Woven fabrics look the same on the front and back.

Woven fabrics, solids, and prints

Scale refers to the size of the design on the fabric. Large-scale designs look different from small-scale designs.

Small-, medium-, and large-scale prints

Fabric that has a design on it has a *visual texture*. How does the fabric look like it would *feel* if you could touch the design? Maybe it would feel smooth like suede or rough like sandpaper.

There are limitless ways to mix colors, values, scales, and visual textures. As you look at quilts, notice how quilters have mixed fabrics. Keep a notebook of ideas. The more ideas you have, the better.

Choosing Fabric for a Quilt

Before we begin a quilt, the first thing we do is figure out what colors we want to work with—what is making us happy right then? We make a stack of fabric for each new quilt. We begin the stack with fabric from our stashes, adding new fabrics from the quilt store as necessary.

When starting your quilt, *you* have to decide what *you* want to use. In some ways, this is like deciding which clothes you want to put on in the morning. It's not necessary to overthink it. Monochromatic (one-color) color schemes are simpler to work with than very colorful, scrappy color schemes. Quilts made from two values (light and dark) are simpler than more complex mixes of values. Look at the quilts in this book as you begin thinking about the colors you want to use. As you choose fabric, don't worry about where you will use each one—that comes later.

Fabric stacks for *Bird on a Branch*, page 38

Once you have decided on colors and selected fabric, separate the background fabrics from the appliqué fabrics. If you have several background fabrics, stack them from darkest to lightest. This is not as hard as it sounds: Look at the fabric in front of you, choose the darkest piece, and start the stack with this piece. Continue choosing the darkest fabric and placing it on the stack. You may or may not be able to use all of the fabrics.

Keep the background in the background.

It is good to have an interesting background, but it is also important to remember that the background is not the quilt's focal point. If you look closely at our pieced backgrounds, you'll notice that the fabrics tend to be similar in color and value. Fabrics that are markedly different are used sparingly.

Next, sort the appliqué fabrics by color. You might have a green stack, an orange stack, a blue stack, and so on. Sort each color from dark to light, as described for the background fabrics. Some fabrics could go in more than one stack. If necessary, you can merge color stacks, blending from one color into another.

You are probably wondering why you are sorting and stacking your fabric. We have found that it is easier to work from an organized group of fabric than it is to work from a disorganized pile. The more you arrange and rearrange the fabric in your stack, the more color combinations you will discover. Plus, it's fun to play with your fabric!

Place your stacks next to each other. Do the background fabrics work with the appliqué fabrics? Do you have the necessary light, medium, and dark values to make your quilt? Are the colors working together? Any fabric that doesn't look good in the stack won't look any better cut up and sewn into your quilt. This is the time to remove any fabric that doesn't work. If a fabric isn't working, force yourself to put it away.

If you have trouble evaluating the fabrics in your stack, stand back and squint or look at them through a reducing glass. Or better yet, take a digital picture of them.

Sometimes you see more in a photo than you do when you're looking at the real thing. Know that this process does get easier with practice.

Design Wall

It is much easier to see how the fabrics are working with each other when you can see them come together on the wall. Design walls can be big and fancy or as simple as a vinyl-backed tablecloth stuck to your wall. For our design walls, we use 4′ × 8′ sheets of 1″-thick foam insulation (available at home improvement stores) covered with batting or flannel. These foam insulation sheets are inexpensive and it is easy to pin into them.

Begin by placing your backgrounds on the design wall (refer to pages 46–47 for more on pieced backgrounds). If something isn't working, now is the time to change it. Begin adding the appliqué fabric in whatever order makes sense to you.

Place all setting blocks, sashing, and borders—all the parts of the quilt—up on the wall. Take a giant step back, and really look at your work. Squint, use a reducing glass, take a picture—do whatever is necessary to help you evaluate your quilt. Only when you are happy with all of your fabric choices should you begin stitching the appliqué.

Leaves in the Breeze, page 21, on the design wall

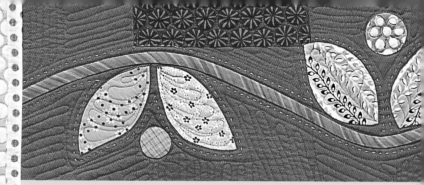

Breaking the Rules

Quilters love rulers and patterns! In the introduction, Becky talked about putting down her ruler to achieve more organic pieced lines in her quilts. That sounds really good, doesn't it? No ruler, no worrying about cutting fabric the wrong size—how great is that? It is great, but it is also different, and different can be uncomfortable.

And patterns! A pattern is your map, your guide—it tells you what to do next and exactly how to do it. Straying from the pattern is not what you have been taught to do, but that is precisely what we are going to encourage you to do. If you are loosening up your piecing, it makes sense to loosen up your appliqué as well.

A good place to start is with *Passion Flowers*. Look at the patterns on the pullout. They are symmetrical and balanced. Now look at the photo of the quilt on page 13. Look at the backgrounds. Look especially at the tulips in the blocks—they point in different angles than do the tulips in the patterns. If you were standing in front of the quilt, you would notice that many shapes vary from the pattern. The leaves and vines in the border are cut freehand and placed by eye—there is no printed border pattern.

This quilt does not feel rigid. Instead, it has a friendly, whimsical air about it that stems directly from the casual appliqué placement and the happy-go-lucky border design.

So loosen up! We'll help you. Before you get started on a project in this book, take a look at Preparing the Backgrounds for Appliqué (pages 46–47), Coping Strips (page 47), Putting Together the Quilt (page 47), Using Templates Loosely (page 54), Using Positioning Overlays Loosely (page 57), and Positioning Appliqué Shapes on the Design Wall (page 58). These sections will give you ideas on how you can loosen up. Most of all, have fun!

Passion Flowers

Finished quilt size: 69″ × 69″

Passion Flowers made by Becky Goldsmith, 2007

This is one of the more conventional quilts in this book. It is a very good quilt to begin letting go of the tools you have learned to rely on.

Becky pieced her block and border backgrounds improvisationally, without rulers. This made the negative space behind the appliqué much more interesting. She used the appliqué templates *as guides*, often drawing outside the lines. She used the positioning overlays for major structural elements, like stems, but placed the majority of the appliqué pieces by eye.

Look at the patterns for the blocks, and you will see that the designs are symmetrical. Look at the finished quilt, however, and you will see that many appliqué shapes are subtly out of position. This is most obvious when you look at the tulips in the blocks. This subtle asymmetry adds whimsy and energy to the quilt.

Becky trimmed the blocks to size without using a ruler. The blocks are *mostly* square and *practically* the same size. Look closely at the sashing strips around the blocks, which were also cut without a ruler, and you will clearly see that the blocks are not perfectly square. The large inner border square unifies the quilt's interior, making the imperfect square blocks look square-er.

Some of you won't want to let go of your rulers; you'll want to follow the pattern exactly. That's fine, too—we are big believers in doing what makes you happy. The following instructions list exact sizes that you can use with your ruler.

There isn't a pattern for the borders. You can work freely or make a paper pattern. Either way, we'll tell you how.

Materials

Refer to our book *The New Appliqué Sampler* and our DVD *Learn to Appliqué the Piece O' Cake Way!* for more complete descriptions of our appliqué techniques.

This is a scrappy quilt. Use the yardage amounts as a guide, as they will vary with the number of fabrics you use. The block and border backgrounds are a combination of reds that are similar in value. Becky used both solids and subtle prints.

Red block backgrounds: A variety of fabrics to total 3 yards

Red border backgrounds: A variety of fabrics to total 2½ yards

Appliqué: A variety of large scraps of fabric

Blue/green vine: A variety of fabrics to total ¾ yard

Yellow sashing: A variety of fabrics to total ½ yard

Blue inner border: A variety of fabrics to total ½ yard

Binding: 1 yard

Backing and sleeve: 5 yards

Batting: 76″ × 76″

Optional: Karen Buckley Perfect Circle templates (refer to Resources on page 64)

Cutting

When cutting without your ruler, you will guesstimate the sizes listed in the project. You can refer to the grid lines on your mat or on a ruler placed nearby—*just don't use the ruler.* If you cut too large a piece, you can trim it later. If you cut too small a piece, you can add to it to bring it up to size (refer to Preparing the Backgrounds for Appliqué on pages 46–47 and Coping Strips on page 47). If you are using a ruler, cut the specific sizes listed below.

Red block background fabrics

Construct 4 squares approximately 26″ × 26″ from a variety of red fabrics **OR** measure and cut 4 squares 26″ × 26″.

Red border background fabrics

From a variety of red fabrics, construct 2 strips approximately 10″ × 56″ for the side borders and 2 strips approximately 10″ × 72″ for the top and bottom borders **OR** cut 2 strips lengthwise 10″ × 56″ for the side borders and 2 strips lengthwise 10″ × 72″ for the top and bottom borders.

Appliqué fabrics

Cut fabric as needed (refer to Block Assembly at right).

Blue/green vine fabrics

Cut several bias strips approximately ⅞″ wide. For a more interesting stem, cut strips from a variety of fabrics. Sew together the strips end-to-end to make a continuous bias stem 340″ long (refer to Organic Bias Stems on page 61) **OR** cut 1 square 20″ × 20″ to make a ⅞″-wide continuous bias strip 340″ long. (Refer to Bias from a Square on page 49.)

Yellow sashing fabrics

Cut 9 or more strips approximately 1½″–2″ × any length to total approximately 360″ **OR** measure and cut 8 strips 1½″ × 40″. *The finished quilt size given is based on 1½″-wide strips.*

Blue inner border fabrics

Cut 8 or more strips approximately 1½″–2″ × any length to total approximately 220″ **OR** measure and cut 6 strips 1½″ × 40″. *The finished quilt size given is based on 1½″-wide strips.*

Binding

Cut 1 square 29″ × 29″ to make a 2½″-wide continuous bias strip 310″ long (refer to page 49).

Block Assembly

Refer to pages 52–58 for instructions on making the templates, making the positioning overlay, and preparing the appliqué. Appliqué patterns are on the pullout at the back of the book.

1. Make templates and a positioning overlay for each block. Note that except for the big flower at the top of each block, the appliqué pieces are the same; they are just used in different places. Therefore, you only need to make *1 template* each for the tulips, leaves, stems, and pot.

2. If you haven't prepared or pieced your backgrounds, do so now (refer to Preparing the Backgrounds for Appliqué on pages 46–47).

3. Press the block backgrounds in half horizontally and vertically. Place the block backgrounds on your design wall.

4. Trace around the appliqué shapes onto the appliqué fabrics (refer to Using Templates Loosely on page 54). Cut out the appliqué pieces for each block, including a ³⁄₁₆″ turn-under allowance. Use the overlay as you choose (refer to Using Positioning Overlays Loosely on page 57), and place the appliqué pieces on the backgrounds on your design wall. Play with your color/fabric choices until you are happy with the way your quilt looks.

Audition the Entire Quilt

It's a good idea to get the entire quilt, including all of the sashing strips and borders (with the border appliqué pieces), on your design wall *before* you begin any stitching.

5. Appliqué the blocks. Finger-press the edges as you go. You may find it helpful to use the Cutaway Appliqué technique (page 59) for the stems.

6. When your appliqué is complete, press each block on the wrong side.

7. Trim blocks to approximately (or exactly if you are using a ruler) 24½″ × 24½″.

Border Assembly

Make a Border Pattern

If you prefer to work from a pattern, draw a rectangle 8″ × 53″ for the side border and 8″ × 69″ for the top border on large pieces of paper. Draw a horizontal and vertical center line on each rectangle.

With a pencil, lightly draw the vine down the center of each pattern, erasing and redrawing the vine as necessary. Cut out leaf shapes from paper, and trace around them on the vine. For the berries, we like to use Karen Buckley's Perfect Circle templates (refer to Resources on page 64), or you can trace a quarter to create the berries on the borders. Make templates and positioning overlays from your finished drawings.

1. If you haven't prepared or pieced the backgrounds for the borders, do so now. Press the border backgrounds in half horizontally and vertically. Place the borders on your design wall around the blocks.

2. Begin with the left side border. Refer to the quilt photo (page 13) as you place the blue/green bias strip lengthwise down the border in a gentle, sinuous curve. Keep the stem close to the center of the border. Pin the stem in place. Repeat for all the border strips.

3. Using scissors or a rotary cutter, cut out leaves for your vine. Becky used her hand as a guide, making the leaves not quite the length from the base of her palm to the tip of her middle finger. Vary the lengths and widths of your leaves. Place the leaves on the wall. Play with the leaf placement until you are happy with the way they look; then pin them in place.

4. Use a chalk pencil to draw circles on the berry fabric. Resist using a circle template. Cut out the circles with a 3⁄16″ turn-under allowance, and place them on the borders.

5. Either remove each border strip and baste the shapes in place, or make a positioning overlay while the borders are still on the design wall (refer to Positioning Appliqué Shapes on the Design Wall on page 58).

6. Appliqué the borders. Finger-press the edges as you go. You may find it helpful to use the Circle Appliqué technique (pages 60–61) for the berries.

7. When your appliqué is complete, press each border on the wrong side.

8. If you are using a ruler, trim the side borders to 8½″ × 53½″. Otherwise, cut the side borders about 8½″ wide; you will trim the length later.

9. If you are using a ruler, trim the top and bottom borders to 8½″ × 69½″. Otherwise, cut these borders about 8½″ wide; you will trim the length later.

Sashing Assembly

If you are using a ruler, sew together the sashing strips end-to-end. Cut:

2 strips 1½″ × 24½″ for A

3 strips 1½″ × 49½″ for B

2 strips 1½″ × 51½″ for C

Inner Border Assembly

If you are using a ruler, sew together the inner border strips end-to-end. Cut:

2 strips 1½″ × 51½″ for the side inner borders

2 strips 1½″ × 53½″ for the top and bottom inner borders

Quilt Assembly

Refer to the Quilt Assembly Diagram and Putting Together the Quilt (page 47).

1. Place the blocks and the outer borders on your design wall. Add the sashing strips and the inner borders. If you are not using a ruler, cut and/or construct sashings and inner borders by eye.

2. Sew a sashing strip A to the bottom of blocks 1 and 2. Add to the sashing strips as necessary. Trim the sashing strip even with the block. (If you are using a ruler, the sashing and inner

border strips should be the correct size already.) Press the seam allowances toward the sashing.

3. Sew blocks 3 and 4 to the sashing strips. Trim or add to the sashing strips as necessary. Press the seam allowances toward the sashing.

4. Sew sashing strips B to the blocks. Trim or add to the sashing strips as necessary. Press the seam allowances toward the sashing.

5. Sew sashing strips C to the top and bottom of the quilt. Trim or add to the sashing strips as necessary. Press the seam allowances toward the sashing.

6. Sew the side inner borders to the quilt. Trim or add to the border strips as necessary. Press the seams toward the inner border.

7. Sew the top and bottom inner borders to the quilt. Trim or add to the border strips as necessary. Press the seams toward the inner border.

8. Center the side borders and sew them to the quilt. Trim them to fit. Press the seams toward the borders.

9. Center the top and bottom borders, and then sew them to the quilt. Trim them to fit. Press the seams toward the borders.

10. Layer and baste the quilt. Quilt by hand or machine (refer to page 48).

11. Finish the quilt (refer to page 48).

Quilt Assembly Diagram

Peppermint Sparkle

Finished quilt size: 46″ × 58″

Peppermint Sparkle made by Becky Goldsmith, 2007

Becky took a block from *Passion Flowers* (page 13), stretched it, and added several flowers from *Tree O' Life* (page 34) to make this perky quilt. There are an infinite number of ways to use the design elements in this book, and we hope that you enjoy trying them out!

Materials

Refer to our book *The New Appliqué Sampler* and our DVD *Learn to Appliqué the Piece O' Cake Way!* for more complete descriptions of our appliqué techniques.

This is a scrappy quilt. Use the yardage amounts as a guide, as they will vary with the number of fabrics you use.

Pink block background: A variety of fabrics to total 1½ yards

Appliqué: A variety of large scraps of fabric

Pink borders: A variety of fabrics to total 1 yard (Notice that Becky used a light pink print on the inside edge of each border strip.)

Binding: ¾ yard

Backing and sleeve: 3¼ yards

Batting: 52″ × 64″

Cutting

When cutting without your ruler, you will guesstimate the sizes listed in the project. You can refer to the grid lines on your mat or on a ruler placed nearby—*just don't use the ruler*. If you cut too large a piece, you can trim it later. If you cut too small a piece, you can add to it to bring it up to size (refer to Preparing the Backgrounds for Appliqué on pages 46–47 and Coping Strips on page 47). If you are using a ruler, cut the specific sizes shown below.

Pink block background fabrics

Construct 1 rectangle approximately 40″ × 51″ from a variety of pink fabrics **OR** measure and cut 1 rectangle 40″ × 51″.

Appliqué fabrics

Cut fabric as needed (refer to Block Assembly below).

Pink border fabrics

From a variety of pink fabrics, construct 2 strips approximately 4½″ × 49½″ for the side borders and 1 strip approximately 4½″ × 46½″ for the top border **OR** measure and cut 4 strips 4½″ × 40″.

Construct 1 strip approximately 5½″ × 46½″ from a variety of pink fabrics for the bottom border **OR** measure and cut 2 strips 5½″ × 40″.

Design Note

Becky cut strips 1½″ wide from a light print and placed them on the inside of each border strip to act as a casual inner border. The 1½″ strips are included in the border width dimensions given.

Binding

Cut 1 square 26″ × 26″ to make a 2½″-wide continuous bias strip 230″ long (refer to page 49).

Block Assembly

Refer to pages 52–58 for instructions on making the templates, making the positioning overlay, and preparing the appliqué. Appliqué patterns are on the pullout at the back of the book.

1. To create a pattern, cut a piece of paper 40″ × 51″, taping pieces of paper together as necessary. Draw a horizontal and vertical center line on the paper.

2. Make a copy of block 2 from *Passion Flowers* (page 13). Cut the block into 2 sections, with the top flower and 2 small leaves on one side of the cut and the rest of the block on the other. Cut the 2 larger tulips away from the bottom section.

3. Place the bottom and top sections on the paper pattern sheet, keeping the stem centered over the vertical center line. The bottom of the pot and the top of the uppermost flower should be approximately 2″ from the edges of the block. Tape the copies in place.

4. Make copies of flowers and leaves from *Tree O' Life* (page 34). Enlarge the patterns as instructed on page 53. Cut out the patterns, and place them on your pattern. This is your quilt, so you get to decide which flowers go where. Once you are happy with the arrangement, tape the copies in place.

5. Make templates and a positioning overlay for the block.

6. If you haven't prepared or pieced your block background, do so now (refer to Preparing the Backgrounds for Appliqué on pages 46–47).

7. Press the block background in half horizontally and vertically. Use a pencil to mark the center lines in the seam allowances. Place the block on your design wall.

8. Trace around the appliqué shapes onto the appliqué fabrics (refer to Using Templates Loosely on page 54). Cut out the appliqué pieces for each block, including a ³⁄₁₆″ turn-under allowance. Use the overlay as you choose (refer to Using Positioning Overlays Loosely on page 57), and place the appliqué pieces on the backgrounds on your design wall. Play with your color/fabric choices until you are happy with the way your quilt looks.

Audition the Entire Quilt

It's a good idea to get the entire quilt, including all of the sashing strips and borders (with the border appliqué pieces), on your design wall *before* you begin any stitching.

9. Appliqué the block. Finger-press the edges as you go. When your appliqué is complete, press the block on the wrong side.

10. Trim the block to approximately (or exactly if you are using a ruler) 38½″ × 49½″.

Quilt Assembly

Refer to the Quilt Assembly Diagram and Putting Together the Quilt (page 47).

1. Sew the side borders to the quilt. Trim or add to the borders as necessary. Press the seams toward the border.

2. Sew the top and bottom borders to the quilt. Trim or add to the borders as necessary. Press the seams toward the inner border.

3. Layer and baste the quilt. Quilt by hand or machine (refer to page 48).

4. Finish the quilt (refer to page 48).

Quilt Assembly Diagram

Leaves in the Breeze

Finished quilt size: 52″ × 60″

Leaves in the Breeze made by Becky Goldsmith, 2007

Take a deep breath. Imagine that you are looking at the blue sky through a screen of leaves that are shimmering in the breeze.

Materials

Refer to our book *The New Appliqué Sampler* and our DVD *Learn to Appliqué the Piece O' Cake Way!* for more complete descriptions of our appliqué techniques.

This is a scrappy quilt. Use the yardage amounts as a guide, as they will vary with the number of fabrics you use.

Blue backgrounds: A variety of fabrics to total 3¾ yards

Appliqué: A variety of large scraps of fabric for the leaves

Orange strips and outer border: A variety of fabrics to total ⅞ yard

Binding: 1 yard

Backing and sleeve: 3¼ yards

Batting: 58″ × 66″

Cutting

When cutting without your ruler, you will guesstimate the sizes listed in the project. You can refer to the grid lines on your mat or on a ruler placed nearby—*just don't use the ruler*. If you cut too large a piece, you can trim it later. If you cut too small a piece, you can add to it to bring it up to size (refer to Preparing the Backgrounds for Appliqué on pages 46–47 and Coping Strips on page 47). If you are using a ruler, cut the specific sizes shown here.

Blue background fabrics

Each row has 11 blocks of varying widths and a finished size of 12″ × 48″.

Cut 55 strips in widths varying from 5″ × 14″ to 9″ × 14″ for a more loosely planned quilt.

OR

Cut 5 strips 7½″ × 14″, and use 1 per row.

Cut 20 strips 6½″ × 14″, and use 4 per row.

Cut 10 strips 6″ × 14″, and use 2 per row.

Cut 20 strips 5″ × 14″, and use 4 per row.

Orange strip fabrics

Cut 30 strips varying from 1″ × 14″ to 3″ × 14″, and use 6 per row **OR** cut 30 strips 1¼″ × 14″, and use 6 per row.

Appliqué fabrics

Cut fabric as needed (refer to Block Assembly on page 23).

Outer borders

Cut 10 or more strips approximately 2½″ × 14″ **OR** measure and cut 10 strips 2½″ × 14″.

Binding

Cut 1 square 29″ × 29″ to make a 2½″-wide continuous bias strip 310″ long (refer to page 49).

Block Assembly

Refer to pages 52–58 for instructions on making the templates, making the positioning overlay, and preparing the appliqué. Leaf template patterns are on page 26.

1. Make templates for the leaves.

2. Place the block backgrounds on your design wall. Number them from left to right and from top to bottom. The top row will have blocks 1 to 11, the next row blocks 12 to 22, and so on.

3. With the blocks placed side by side on the design wall, measure the width of the rows. Each row should be close to 70″ wide.

4. Before you start, refer to Preparing the Backgrounds for Appliqué on pages 46–47. These block backgrounds meet at odd angles. To cut these angles, place block backgrounds 1 and 2 right sides up on your rotary mat. Line up their baselines with a line on the mat. Overlap the edges 1″–2″.

Note

If you prefer to keep your blocks straight, without angled lines, skip Steps 4–6 and go to Step 7.

Place blocks 1 and 2 on your mat. Overlap them, and align baselines.

5. Choose an angle, and cut a line in the area where the block backgrounds overlap. Discard the excess fabric.

Cut angled line where blocks 1 and 2 overlap.

Notes About Angled Lines

The edges of each row should remain at 90° angles.

The angled cuts do not need to be extreme; subtle tilting is fine.

Balance the angles. Too many angles to the right (or left) will feel off balance.

Do not trim away too much fabric. Blocks can be cut down to size later.

6. Return block background 1 to your design wall. Leave block background 2 on your mat. Take block background 3 from your design wall, and place it to the right of block background 2. Line up the baselines, and overlap the edges where the blocks meet. Choose an angle, and cut a line in the area where the backgrounds overlap.

Cut angled line where blocks 2 and 3 overlap.

7. Repeat Steps 5 and 6 until all the block backgrounds are trimmed to your liking.

8. Refer to Using Templates Loosely (page 54). Each block has 4 leaves. The bases of these leaves grow out of the seam allowance on either the block's right or left side. This is the leaf-edge side of the block.

9. Mix and match leaf templates. Cut out the leaves with their turn-under allowances. Place the leaves on each block background on your design wall. Leaves can be placed in any orientation and in any order on the blocks.

10. Place the orange strips on the design wall. Play with their size and placement.

11. Place the outer border strips on each side of the quilt.

12. Appliqué the blocks. Finger-press the edges as you go. Place the bases of the leaves about ¼″ from the leaf-edge side of the block. Notice that some leaves extend into the seams more than others do. Leave at least 1″ on each of the other 3 sides of the block free of leaves.

Note

You do not need to turn under the point of the leaf that is sewn into the seam on the leaf-edge side. Handle the angled edges of the block carefully when sewing.

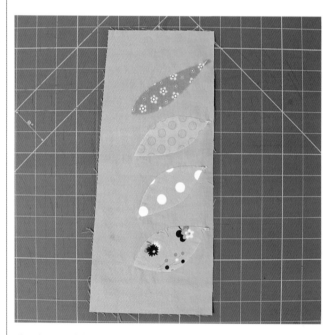

Place leaves ¼″ from leaf-edge side of block. Do not turn point at base of leaves.

13. When your appliqué is complete, press the blocks on the wrong side.

14. Follow the established angle at the edges of the blocks to trim away ¼″–½″ on the leaf-edge side of each block. Trim the top and bottom edges of the block, making it about 12½″ tall. Cut by eye, or use a ruler on the leaf-edge side.

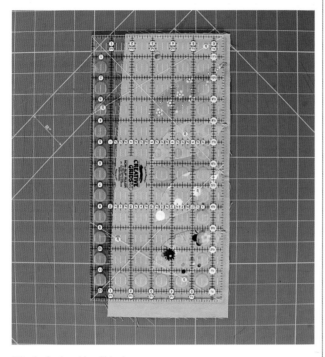

Trim leaf-edge side of block.

Before trimming the non-leaf-edge side of each block, evaluate the length of the rows. Trim this edge by eye, taking off more fabric where there seems to be too much open space. Some of these edges may not require trimming.

OR

If you are maintaining straight edges on your blocks, cut your blocks as follows:

If your block background was 7½″ × 14″, trim it to 6″ × 12½″.

If your block background was 6½″ × 14″, trim it to 5″ × 12½″.

If your block background was 6″ × 14″, trim it to 4½″ × 12½″.

If your block background was 5″ × 14″, trim it to 3½″ × 12½″.

Quilt Assembly

Refer to the Quilt Assembly Diagram and Putting Together the Quilt (page 47).

1. Sew the blocks into pairs, inserting the orange strips as you go. Press seam allowances in either direction. Trim away the ends of the orange strips that extend beyond the top and bottom of the row.

2. Sew the pairs of blocks together. Press seam allowances in either direction. Gradually sew the blocks into rows, trimming or adding fabric as necessary, making 5 rows 12½″ × 48½″.

3. Sew the 5 rows together.

4. Sew the side border strips together. Cut into 2 strips 2½″ × 60½″.

5. Sew the left side border to the quilt. Press to the border. Sew the right side border to the quilt. Press to the border.

6. Layer and baste the quilt. Quilt by hand or machine (refer to page 48).

7. Finish the quilt (refer to page 48).

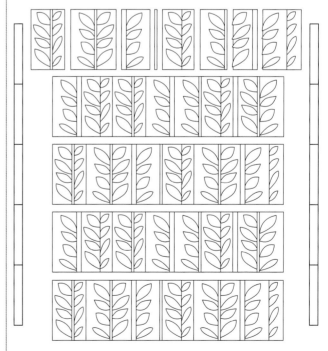

Quilt Assembly Diagram

Leaf Templates

5

12

10

6

3

7

2

8

1

9

4

11

Appliqué Outside the Lines

Picasso's Garden

Picasso's Garden made by Becky Goldsmith, 2007

Vines are a perennial favorite in appliqué designs. Becky has created a modern variation of the classic vine—with Cubist-looking leaves and fluid lines. It's very obvious that Becky did not use a ruler when constructing this quilt. *Picasso's Garden* was built on her design wall.

Materials

Refer to our book *The New Appliqué Sampler* and our DVD *Learn to Appliqué the Piece O' Cake Way!* for more complete descriptions of our appliqué techniques.

This is a scrappy quilt. Use the yardage amounts as a guide, as they will vary with the number of fabrics you use. The panel backgrounds are a combination of browns that are similar in value.

Brown background: A variety of fabrics to total 2¾ yards

Appliqué: A variety of large scraps of blue fabrics.

Blue/green vine: A variety of fabrics to total ½ yard

Green sashing: A variety of fabrics to total ⅝ yard

Binding: ¾ yard

Backing and sleeve: 3¼ yards

Batting: 55" × 63"

Cutting

When cutting without your ruler, you will guesstimate the sizes listed in the project. You can refer to the grid lines on your mat or on a ruler placed nearby—*just don't use the ruler.* If you cut too large a piece, you can trim it later. If you cut too small a piece, you can add to it to bring it up to size (refer to Preparing the Backgrounds for Appliqué on pages 46–47 and Coping Strips on page 47). If you are using a ruler, cut the specific sizes shown here.

Brown background fabrics

Construct 3 backgrounds from a variety of brown fabrics that are approximately

17" × 59" for A

15" × 59" for B

16" × 59" for C

OR measure and cut 3 backgrounds using the exact measurements listed above.

Appliqué fabrics

Cut fabric as needed (refer to Block Assembly on page 29).

Refer to the quilt photo (page 27) and the Quilt Assembly Diagram (page 29) to cut rectangles for leaves and triangles and circles for flowers.

Blue/green vine fabrics

Cut several bias strips approximately ⅞" wide. For a more interesting stem, cut strips from a variety of fabrics. Sew together the strips end-to-end to make a continuous bias stem 200" long (refer to Organic Bias Stems on page 61) **OR** cut 1 square 16" × 16" to make a ⅞"-wide continuous bias strip 200" long (refer to Bias from a Square on page 49).

Green sashing fabrics

Construct 2 strips each from a variety of fabrics that are approximately

2" × 57½" for D

2½" × 57½" for E

OR measure and cut 2 strips each using the exact measurements listed above.

Binding

Cut 1 square 26" × 26" to make a 2½"-wide continuous bias strip 240" long (refer to page 49).

Block Assembly

Refer to pages 52–58 for instructions on making the positioning overlay and preparing the appliqué.

1. If you haven't prepared or pieced your backgrounds, do so now (refer to Preparing the Backgrounds for Appliqué, pages 46–47). Press the backgrounds, and place them on your design wall.

2. Beginning with the vines, place the appliqué pieces on the backgrounds on your design wall.

3. The leaves are simple rectangles and triangles that can be cut by hand, without templates. Becky used her hand as a guide to cut rectangles that are roughly 2″ wide and 4″–8″ long. Cut the leaves, and put them on your backgrounds. Cut triangles to fit your space. Use a quarter for the circle template. Remember to add turn-under allowances to all appliqué pieces. Play with your color/fabric choices until you are happy with the way your quilt looks.

4. Place sashing strips D and E in place on your design wall.

Audition the Entire Quilt

It's a good idea to get the entire quilt, including the sashing strips, on your design wall *before* you begin any stitching.

5. Either remove each panel and baste the shapes in place, or make a positioning overlay while the borders are still on the design wall (refer to Positioning Appliqué Shapes on the Design Wall on page 58).

6. Appliqué each panel. Finger-press the edges as you go. When your appliqué is complete, press each panel on the wrong side.

7. Trim the panels to approximately (or exactly if you are using a ruler)

  15½″ × 57½″ for A

  13½″ × 57½″ for B

  14½″ × 57½″ for C

Quilt Assembly

Refer to the Quilt Assembly Diagram and Putting Together the Quilt (page 47).

1. Place the panels and sashing strips on your design wall.

2. Sew the panels together with sashing strips D between them. Trim or add to the sashing strips as necessary. Press seam allowances toward the D strips.

3. Sew sashing strips E to the sides of the quilt. Trim or add to the sashing strips as necessary. Press the seam allowances toward the E strips.

4. Layer and baste the quilt. Quilt by hand or machine (refer to page 48).

5. Finish the quilt (refer to page 48).

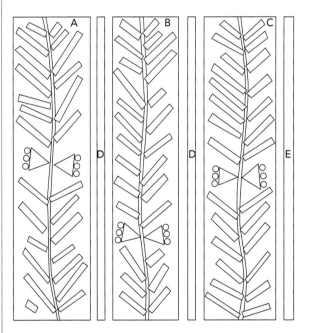

Quilt Assembly Diagram

The Ground
(as Seen from Above)

Finished quilt size: 65″ × 33″

The Ground (as Seen from Above) made by Becky Goldsmith, 2007

Materials

Refer to our book *The New Appliqué Sampler* and our DVD *Learn to Appliqué the Piece O' Cake Way!* for more complete descriptions of our appliqué techniques.

This is a scrappy quilt. Use the yardage amounts as a guide, as they will vary with the number of fabrics you use.

Green block backgrounds and border: A variety of fabrics to total 2¼ yards

Appliqué: A variety of large scraps of fabric (Becky used woven plaids and stripes from Guatemala.)

Light border: A variety of fabrics to total ⅞ yard

Binding: ⅞ yard

Backing and sleeve: 2½ yards

Batting: 71″ × 39″

Have you ever looked out of an airplane window and seen irrigation circles in the farmland far below? Those circles, marks of a farmer's hard work and of the crops that feed us all, were the inspiration for this quilt.

Cutting

When cutting without your ruler, you will guesstimate the sizes listed in the project. You can refer to the grid lines on your mat or on a ruler placed nearby—*just don't use the ruler.* If you cut too large a piece, you can trim it later. If you cut too small a piece, you can add to it to bring it up to size (refer to Preparing the Backgrounds for Appliqué on pages 46–47 and Coping Strips on page 47). If you are using a ruler, cut the specific sizes shown here.

Green background fabrics

The background is broken into 3 sections, making it easier to appliqué (refer to the Quilt Assembly Diagram on page 32).

Construct 3 backgrounds from a variety of green fabrics that are approximately

19½″ × 27″ for A
22″ × 27″ for B
21½″ × 27″ for C

OR measure and cut 3 backgrounds in the exact measurements listed above.

Appliqué fabrics

Cut fabric as needed (refer to Block Assembly below).

Green border fabrics

Cut 72 strips varying from 1″ × 4½″ to 3″ × 4½″ (approximately or exactly) from a variety of green fabrics for the borders.

Light border fabrics

Cut 72 strips varying from 1″ × 4½″ to 3″ × 4½″ (approximately or exactly) from a variety of light fabrics for the borders.

Binding

Cut 1 square 26″ × 26″ to make a 2½″-wide continuous bias strip 226″ long (refer to page 49).

Block Assembly

Refer to pages 52–58 for instructions on making the templates, making the positioning overlay, and preparing the appliqué. Appliqué template patterns are on page 33.

1. Make templates for the circles. The wedges are very simple shapes that can easily be cut without templates. Refer to the patterns to cut yours by hand, or if you prefer, make templates for the wedges, adding a ³⁄₁₆″ turn-under allowance.

tip If you do make templates, note that in each wheel, the same wedge is repeated seven to nine times. You only need one wedge template per wheel.

2. If you haven't prepared or pieced your backgrounds, do so now (refer to Preparing the Backgrounds for Appliqué on pages 46–47). Press the backgrounds, and place them on your design wall.

3. Cut out the appliqué pieces, adding turn-under allowances. Place the appliqué pieces on the backgrounds on your design wall. Play with your color/fabric choices until you are happy with the way your quilt looks. Randomly scatter the small circles on the blocks.

Audition the Entire Quilt

It's a good idea to get the entire quilt, including the sashing strips, on your design wall *before* you begin any stitching.

4. Either remove each block and baste the shapes in place, or make a positioning overlay while the borders are still on the design wall (refer to Positioning Appliqué Shapes on the Design Wall on page 58).

Note

Wheel 11 is appliquéd after the borders are sewn to the quilt.

5. Appliqué the blocks. Finger-press the edges as you go. When your appliqué is complete, press each block on the wrong side.

6. Trim the blocks to approximately (or exactly if you are using a ruler)

18″ × 25½″ for A
20½″ × 25½″ for B
20″ × 25½″ for C

Border Assembly

1. Alternate green and light strips for the borders. Vary the widths of the strips:

Make 2 strips 4½″ × 57½″ approximately (or exactly if you are using a ruler) for the top and bottom borders.

Make 2 strips 4½″ × 33½″ approximately (or exactly if you are using a ruler) for the side borders.

2. Press the seam allowances toward the green strips.

Quilt Assembly

Refer to the Quilt Assembly Diagram and Putting Together the Quilt (page 47).

1. Place the blocks and borders on your design wall.

2. Sew the blocks together, and press.

3. Sew the top and bottom borders to the quilt. Trim or add to the border strips as necessary. Press the seams toward the border.

4. Sew the side borders to the quilt. Trim or add to the border strips as necessary. Press the seams toward the border.

5. Appliqué wheel 11, taking care not to stretch the outer edges of the quilt. Press.

6. Layer and baste the quilt. Quilt by hand or machine (refer to page 48).

7. Finish the quilt (refer to page 48).

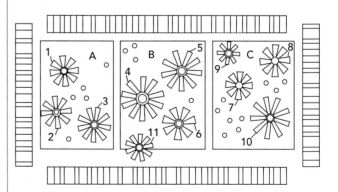

Quilt Assembly Diagram

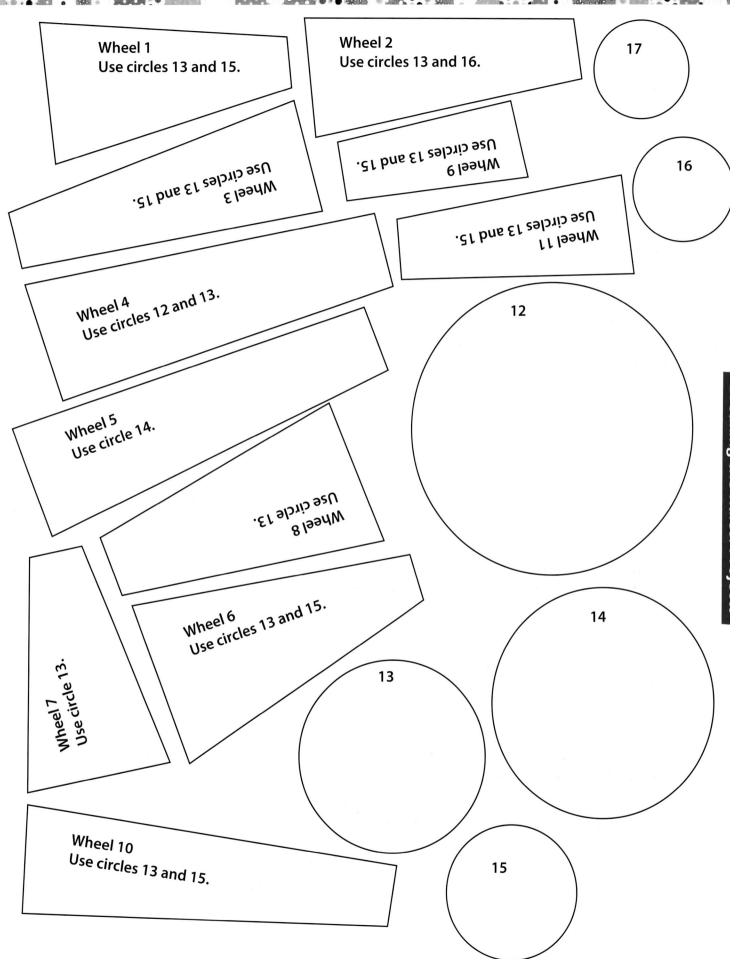

Wheel 1
Use circles 13 and 15.

Wheel 2
Use circles 13 and 16.

17

Wheel 3
Use circles 13 and 15.

Wheel 9
Use circles 13 and 15.

16

Wheel 11
Use circles 13 and 15.

Wheel 4
Use circles 12 and 13.

12

Wheel 5
Use circle 14.

Wheel 8
Use circle 13.

Wheel 6
Use circles 13 and 15.

14

Wheel 7
Use circle 13.

13

Wheel 10
Use circles 13 and 15.

15

The Ground (As Seen from Above)

Tree O' Life

Finished quilt size: 64″ × 66″

Tree O' Life made by Becky Goldsmith, 2007

The farther you are from things, the grayer (and sometimes bluer) they appear to be. One way to imply distance in your quilts is to use grayer colors in the background. Cleaner, crisper colors come forward visually and stand out against a grayer background. Have you ever thought about why colors in the distance appear to be grayer than colors that are closer to you? It's because there is stuff (dirt, dust, water, and so on) in the air between you and what you are looking at.

Look at the colors Becky used in this quilt. The pieced strips in the background behind the tree are very gray shades of gold. The border backgrounds are a little less gray, and the greens are cleaner, especially toward the bottom of the quilt. This is why the background behind the tree appears to be farther away than the border backgrounds. The clean, lively colors of the appliqué come forward. This effect was planned—it was not an accident.

All of the pieced lines in the block and border backgrounds, including the outer edges of the quilt, were cut without using a ruler. Becky *was* very careful when trimming the outer edges. She folded the quilt in half in both directions in an effort to keep the edges more or less equal in length.

Materials

Refer to our book *The New Appliqué Sampler* and our DVD *Learn to Appliqué the Piece O' Cake Way!* for more complete descriptions of our appliqué techniques.

This is a scrappy quilt. Use the yardage amounts as a guide, as they will vary with the number of fabrics you use.

Gold background: A variety of fabrics to total 1½–1¾ yards

Green/gold border backgrounds: A variety of fabrics to total 2¾ yards

Appliqué: A variety of large scraps of fabric

Brown vine in bottom border: ½ yard

Binding: 1 yard

Backing and sleeve: 4¾ yards

Batting: 70″ × 72″

Cutting

When cutting without your ruler, you will guesstimate the sizes listed in the project. You can refer to the grid lines on your mat or on a ruler placed nearby—*just don't use the ruler*. If you cut too large a piece, you can trim it later. If you cut too small a piece, you can add to it to bring it up to size (refer to Preparing the Backgrounds for Appliqué on pages 46–47 and Coping Strips on page 47). If you are using a ruler, cut the specific sizes shown here.

Gold background fabrics
Construct a quilt center approximately 44½″ × 54½″ from a variety of strips of gold fabrics **OR** measure and cut 1 rectangle 44½″ × 54½″.

Left side border
Construct 1 strip approximately 14″ × 52″ from a variety of green and gold fabrics **OR** measure and cut 1 strip 14″ × 52″.

Top border
Construct 1 strip approximately 10″ × 44″ from a variety of green and gold fabrics **OR** measure and cut 1 strip 10″ × 44″.

Right side border
Construct 1 strip approximately 14″ × 60″ from a variety of green and gold fabrics **OR** measure and cut 1 strip 14″ × 60″.

Bottom border fabrics

Construct 1 strip approximately 10″ × 66″ from a variety of green and gold fabrics **OR** measure and cut 1 strip 10″ × 66″.

Brown vine fabric for the bottom border

Cut several bias strips approximately ⅞″ wide. Sew the strips together end-to-end to make a continuous bias stem 100″ long (refer to Organic Bias Stems on page 61).

Appliqué fabrics

Cut fabric as needed (refer to Block Assembly below).

Binding

Cut 1 square 29″ × 29″ to make a 2½″-wide continuous bias strip 310″ long (refer to page 49).

Block Assembly

Refer to pages 52–58 for instructions on making the templates, making the positioning overlay, and preparing the appliqué. Appliqué patterns are on the pullout at the back of the book.

Note

Enlarge pattern 50% before using.

1. Make templates and a positioning overlay for the block. Note that many of the templates are large (refer to Making Big Templates on page 53).

2. If you haven't prepared or pieced your background, do so now (refer to Preparing the Backgrounds for Appliqué on pages 46–47).

3. Press the block background in half horizontally and vertically. Place the background on your design wall.

4. Trace around the appliqué shapes onto the appliqué fabrics (refer to Using Templates Loosely on page 54). Cut out the appliqué pieces for each block, including a ³⁄₁₆″ turn-under allowance. Use the overlay on the wall if you choose (refer to Using Positioning Overlays Loosely on page 57), and place the appliqué pieces on the back-

grounds on your design wall. Play with your color/fabric choices until you are happy with the way your quilt looks.

Audition the Entire Quilt

It's a good idea to get the entire quilt, including the border, on your design wall *before* you begin any stitching.

5. You may find it helpful to use the Cutaway Appliqué technique (page 59) on the stems as you appliqué the block.

6. Refer to Border Assembly below as you put the border backgrounds and appliqué pieces on your design wall to audition the complete design.

7. Appliqué the block. Finger-press the edges as you go. When your appliqué is complete, press the block on the wrong side.

8. Trim the quilt center to approximately (or exactly if you are using a ruler) 40½″ × 50½″.

Border Assembly

1. Make templates and positioning overlays for the borders.

2. If you haven't prepared or pieced your border backgrounds, do so now. Press the border backgrounds in half horizontally and vertically. Place the borders on your design wall around the block.

3. Trace around the appliqué shapes onto the appliqué fabrics (refer to Using Templates Loosely on page 54). Cut out the appliqué pieces for each block, including a ³⁄₁₆″ turn-under allowance. Use the overlay as you choose (refer to Using Positioning Overlays Loosely on page 57), and place the appliqué pieces on the backgrounds on your design wall. Refer to the project photo (page 34) as necessary. Play with your color/fabric choices until you are happy with the way your quilt looks.

4. Make an organic bias stem for the vine on the bottom border (refer to Organic Bias Stems on page 61).

5. Appliqué the borders. Finger-press the edges as you go. Note that some of the appliqué pieces in the upper left of the right border are appliquéd after the borders are sewn to the quilt. You may find it helpful to use the Cutaway Appliqué technique (page 59) on the words in the top border and on the narrow stems.

6. When your appliqué is complete, press each border on the wrong side.

7. If you are using a ruler, trim the left side border to 12½″ × 50½″. Otherwise, cut this border about 12½″ wide. You will trim the length later.

8. If you are using a ruler, trim the top border to 8½″ × 52½″. Otherwise, cut this border about 8½″ wide. You will trim the length later.

9. If you are using a ruler, trim the right side border to 12½″ × 58½″. Otherwise, cut this border about 12½″ wide. You will trim the length later.

10. If you are using a ruler, trim the bottom border to 8½″ × 64½″. Otherwise, cut this border about 8½″ wide. You will trim the length later.

Quilt Assembly

Refer to the Quilt Assembly Diagram and Putting Together the Quilt (page 47).

1. Place the quilt center and borders on your design wall. Sew the left side border to the quilt. Press the seams toward the border.

2. Sew the top border to the quilt. Press the seams toward the border.

3. Sew the right side border to the quilt. Press the seams toward the border.

4. Sew the bottom border to the quilt. Press the seams toward the border.

5. Finish the appliqué in the right border.

6. Layer and baste the quilt. Quilt by hand or machine (refer to page 48).

7. Finish the quilt (refer to page 48).

Piping

Becky used piping in the seam between the quilt and the binding. This is a nice way to add a little detail of color. Becky used the continuous bias from a square technique (page 49) to make continuous bias strips and then used Susan Cleveland's Piping Hot Binding Tool (available at www.pieceocake.com) to make the piping and binding.

Quilt Assembly Diagram

Bird on a Branch

Finished quilt size: 20˝ × 54˝

Bird on a Branch made by Linda Jenkins, 2008

Here's an idea! Linda made this cute wall quilt using just the left side border from *Tree O' Life* (page 34). There are an infinite number of ways to use the many design elements in this book.

Materials

Refer to our book *The New Appliqué Sampler* and our DVD *Learn to Appliqué the Piece O' Cake Way!* for more complete descriptions of our appliqué techniques.

This is a scrappy quilt. Use the yardage amounts as a guide, as they will vary with the number of fabrics you use.

Orange block background: A variety of fabrics to total 1 yard

Appliqué: A variety of large scraps of fabric

Orange print border: ½ yard

Maroon inner border: ¼ yard

Binding: ¾ yard

Backing and sleeve: 1⅝ yard

Batting: 26″ × 62″

Cutting

When cutting without your ruler, you will guesstimate the sizes listed in the project. You can refer to the grid lines on your mat or on a ruler placed nearby—*just don't use the ruler.* If you cut too large a piece, you can trim it later. If you cut too small a piece, you can add to it to bring it up to size (refer to Preparing the Backgrounds for Appliqué on pages 46–47 and Coping Strips on page 47). If you are using a ruler, cut the specific sizes shown here.

Orange block background fabrics

Construct 1 rectangle approximately 14″ × 52″ from a variety of orange fabrics **OR** measure and cut 1 rectangle 14″ × 52″.

Appliqué fabrics

Cut fabric as needed (refer to Block Assembly below).

Orange print border fabric

Cut 4 strips approximately (or exactly if you are using a ruler) 3½″ × 40″.

Maroon inner border fabric

Cut 4 strips approximately (or exactly if you are using a ruler) 1¼″ × 40″.

Binding

Cut 1 square 22″ × 22″ to make a 2½″-wide continuous bias strip 180″ long (refer to page 49).

Block Assembly

Refer to pages 52–58 for instructions on making the templates, making the positioning overlay, and preparing the appliqué. Appliqué patterns are on the pullout at the back of the book.

1. Use the pattern for the left side border from *Tree O' Life* to make templates and overlays for the block. Enlarge the patterns as instructed on page 53.

2. If you haven't prepared or pieced your background, do so now (refer to Preparing the Backgrounds for Appliqué on pages 46–47).

3. Press the block background in half horizontally and vertically. Place the background on your design wall.

4. Trace around the appliqué shapes onto the appliqué fabrics (refer to Using Templates Loosely on page 54). Cut out the appliqué pieces for each block, including a ³⁄₁₆″ turn-under allowance. Use the overlay as you choose (refer to Using Positioning Overlays Loosely on page 57), and place the appliqué pieces on the backgrounds on your design wall. Play with your color/fabric choices until you are happy with the way your quilt looks.

Audition the Entire Quilt

It's a good idea to get the entire quilt, including the sashing strips, on your design wall *before* you begin any stitching.

5. Appliqué the block. Finger-press the edges as you go. When your appliqué is complete, press the block on the wrong side.

6. Trim the block to approximately (or exactly if you are using a ruler) 12½″ × 50½″.

Border Assembly

1. Sew together the inner border strips end-to-end. Cut approximately (or exactly if you are using a ruler):

2 strips 1¼″ × 50½″ for the side borders

2 strips 1¼″ × 14″ for the top and bottom borders

2. Sew together the border strips end-to-end. Cut approximately (or exactly if you are using a ruler):

2 strips 3½″ × 52″ for the side borders

2 strips 3½″ × 20″ for the top and bottom borders

Quilt Assembly

Refer to the Quilt Assembly Diagram and Putting Together the Quilt (page 47).

1. Sew the side inner borders to the quilt. Trim or add to the inner border strips as necessary. Press the seams toward the inner border.

2. Sew the top and bottom inner borders to the quilt. Trim or add to the inner border strips as necessary. Press the seams toward the inner border.

3. Sew the side borders to the quilt. Trim or add to the border strips as necessary. Press the seams toward the border.

4. Sew the top and bottom borders to the quilt. Trim or add to the border strips as necessary. Press the seams toward the border.

5. Layer and baste the quilt. Quilt by hand or machine (refer to page 48).

6. Finish the quilt (refer to page 48).

Quilt Assembly Diagram

Tulips Gone Wild

Finished quilt size: 64″ × 64″

Tulips Gone Wild made by Linda Jenkins, quilted by Mary Covey, 2008

Linda set together a variety of yellow prints in large Roman stripe blocks for the background of this quilt. She repeated the tulip branch from *Tree O' Life* (page 34) four times around a pointy center sunflower. The slightly off-center wavy strips on the borders are a soft counterpoint to the angularity of the tulips.

Materials

Refer to our book *The New Appliqué Sampler* and our DVD *Learn to Appliqué the Piece O' Cake Way!* for more complete descriptions of our appliqué techniques.

This is a scrappy quilt. Use the yardage amounts as a guide, as they will vary with the number of fabrics you use.

Yellow block backgrounds: A variety of fabrics to total 3 yards

Appliqué: A variety of large scraps of fabric

Red borders: 1⅜ yards

Yellow borders: 1 yard

Binding: 1 yard

Backing and sleeve: 4 yards

Batting: 70″ × 70″

Cutting

When cutting without your ruler, you will guesstimate the sizes listed in the project. You can refer to the grid lines on your mat or on a ruler placed nearby—*just don't use the ruler*. If you cut too large a piece, you can trim it later. If you cut too small a piece, you can add to it to bring it up to size (refer to Preparing the Backgrounds for Appliqué on pages 46–47 and Coping Strips on page 47). If you are using a ruler, cut the specific sizes shown here.

Yellow block background fabrics

Cut 64 strips approximately (or exactly if you are using a ruler) 4″ × 14½″ from a variety of yellow fabrics

Appliqué fabrics

Cut fabric as needed (refer to Block Assembly below).

Red border fabric

Cut 7 strips approximately (or exactly if you are using a ruler) 6″ × 40″.

Yellow border fabric

Cut 7 strips approximately (or exactly if you are using a ruler) 4″ × 40″.

Binding

Cut 1 square 28″ × 28″ to make a 2½″-wide continuous bias strip 280″ long (refer to page 49).

Block Assembly

Refer to pages 52–58 for instructions on making the templates, making the positioning overlay, and preparing the appliqué. Appliqué patterns are on the pullout at the back of the book.

1. To create a pattern, cut a piece of paper 28″ × 28″, taping pieces of paper together as necessary. Draw a horizontal and vertical center line on the paper.

2. Make a copy of the tulip branch from the *Tree O' Life* pattern. Enlarge as directed on page 53.

3. Place the copy on the paper pattern sheet. The primary stem is positioned at nearly a 45° angle on the pattern. The outermost points of the tulips should be 1″–2″ from the edges of the block. Tape the copy in place on the pattern sheet. Redraw the center lines as necessary.

4. Draw a pointy center flower that is roughly 7″ in diameter for the center of the quilt. This flower will cover the ends of the branches.

5. Make templates and a positioning overlay for the block and the center flower.

6. For each block background, sew 4 strips together to make a 14½″ × 14½″ square. Repeat to assemble 3 more squares. (Refer to Preparing the Backgrounds for Appliqué on pages 46–47.) Sew 4 squares together to make 1 block background. Press the background in half horizontally and vertically.

7. Repeat Step 6 to make 4 block backgrounds.

Block Background

8. Trace around the appliqué shapes onto the appliqué fabrics (refer to Using Templates Loosely on page 54). Cut out the appliqué pieces for each block, including a ³⁄₁₆″ turn-under allowance. Use the overlay as you choose (refer to Using Positioning Overlays Loosely on page 57), and place the appliqué pieces on the backgrounds on your design wall. Play with your color/fabric choices until you are happy with the way your quilt looks.

tip

Notice that one leaf falls off each block. Appliqué that end of the leaf *after* the blocks have been set together.

Audition the Entire Quilt

It's a good idea to get the entire quilt, including the sashing strips, on your design wall *before* you begin any stitching.

9. Appliqué the blocks. Finger-press as you go. When your appliqué is complete, press the blocks on the wrong side.

10. Your blocks should measure approximately (or exactly if you are using a ruler) 28½″ × 28½″. If you need to trim the outer edges a bit to clean them up, do so now. Depending on how much you cut, you may need to reduce the length of your borders.

Border Assembly

1. Sew together the red border strips end-to-end. Cut approximately (or exactly if you are using a ruler):

2 strips 6″ × 58″ for the side borders

2 strips 6″ × 66″ for the top and bottom borders

2. Sew together the yellow border strips end-to-end. Cut approximately (or exactly if you are using a ruler):

2 strips 4″ × 58″ for the side borders

2 strips 4″ × 66″ for the top and bottom borders

3. The wavy strip of yellow fabric on each outer border is drawn by hand. On the yellow border fabric, draw the 2 lines that mark the edges of the wavy line.

4. Finger-press and then baste the yellow strip on top of a red border strip. Use the Cutaway Appliqué technique (page 59) to appliqué the strip in place. Repeat for all the borders.

5. Press the borders on the wrong side. Trim the side borders to approximately (or exactly if you are using a ruler) 4½″ × 56½″.

6. Trim the top and bottom borders to approximately (or exactly if you are using a ruler) 4½″ × 64½″.

Quilt Assembly

Refer to the Quilt Assembly Diagram and Putting Together the Quilt (page 47).

1. Sew the 4 block backgrounds together, and trim or add to them as necessary. Finish appliquéing the ends of the leaves. Appliqué the center flower to the quilt. Press.

2. Sew the side borders to the quilt. Trim or add to the border strips as necessary. Press the seams toward the border.

3. Sew the top and bottom borders to the quilt. Trim or add to the border strips as necessary. Press the seams toward the border.

4. Layer and baste the quilt. Quilt by hand or machine (refer to page 48).

5. Finish the quilt (refer to page 48).

Quilt Assembly Diagram

Appliqué Outside the Lines

Fabric Preparation

Prewash your fabric before using it. Prewashing is a good way to test for colorfastness and shrinkage. It is better that the fabric bleed or shrink *before* it is sewn into the quilt. Prewashed fabric also has a better hand, and it smells better. In addition, washing removes the chemicals that some people are allergic to. Finally, prewashed fabric appliqués better because it frays less.

We wash cotton fabric in the washing machine using Orvus Paste or Quilt Soap. Both can be found online. Orvus Paste is a neutral synthetic detergent that can be bought by the gallon. It is soluble in both hot and cold water and rinses out freely. It is intended to be used on animals large and small—and it is wonderful for your cotton fabric. Use 1 to 2 tablespoons of Orvus Paste per washer load.

It's a good idea to have Synthrapol detergent and Retayne fixative on hand. Synthrapol is a product that you add to wash water to keep any dye molecules that come out of the fabric from redepositing back into the fabric. Retayne helps keep the dye molecules in the fabric to begin with. Because water chemistry varies, it is important that you experiment a little to find out how these products work best for you. You can also use the Color Catcher sheets made by Shout. In any case, follow the manufacturer's instructions.

Dry the cotton fabric in the dryer on warm. Do not add a dryer sheet, because it will add softness to the fabric, which makes the fabric a little harder to handle. Remove fabric from the dryer while it is still a little warm. Smooth out wrinkles, and fold it to fit your shelf or drawer. It is not necessary to press fabric at this point. You *will* need to press it before you cut it.

About Our Fabric Requirements

Cotton fabric is usually 40" to 44" wide off the bolt. To be safe, we calculate all of our fabric requirements based on a 40" width.

Use the fabric requirements for each quilt as a guide, but remember that the yardage amounts vary depending on how many fabrics you use and the sizes of the pieces you cut. Our measurements allow for both fabric shrinkage and a few errors in cutting.

General Instructions

About Seam Allowances

All machine piecing is designed for ¼" seam allowances.

Preparing the Backgrounds for Appliqué

When you begin cutting fabric with only your rotary mat and cutter, it will be hard not to grab the ruler. "I'll just use the ruler for a little bit," you might think to yourself. The more you use the ruler, though, the less likely you are to let go of it. Our advice is this . . . *Don't touch the ruler!* Hide it from yourself. Force yourself to cut freely. The more you don't use it, the easier it gets.

The Helpful Grid

Your rotary mat has a gridded side and a plain side. It is helpful to use the gridded side and to refer to the grid when you cut. The lines will help you estimate the size of the piece you are cutting.

CUTTING AND SEWING

The technique used in this book is a lot like crazy piecing. There is no pattern. You sew together the fabrics until you have a background that is *at least* 2" wider and 2" longer than you need. It is a good idea to look at the backgrounds on your design wall as you build them.

1. Place your largest rotary mat on the table. Make sure your fabric has been pressed, as it's hard to work with wrinkled or creased fabric.

2. Place a piece of fabric right side up on the mat. Place the second piece of fabric right side up on top of the first piece of fabric. Align the top edges of the 2 pieces. Overlap one edge of each piece of fabric enough so that when you cut, you cut through both pieces of fabric at once.

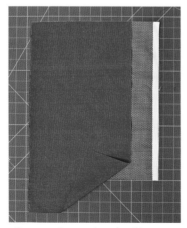

Align top edges, and overlap fabric.

3. Use your rotary cutter to cut through both fabrics. Your cut can be straight or a little bit curved. If you do cut curved lines, be sure to cut very gentle curves—no U-turns! Gentle curves are easier to match and don't require clipping.

Cut through both fabrics.

4. Remove the excess fabric.

5. The 2 pieces are now cut to match. Place the fabrics right sides together, aligning the top edges. Pin and then sew them together with a ¼" seam allowance.

Pin and sew.

Concave Side Up

To avoid sewing pleats into curved seams, it is best to sew with the concave side up.

6. Add another fabric to any side of the 2 fabrics you have sewn together. Overlap the new fabric with the first unit, as you did in Step 2. Cut through all fabrics. Discard the excess fabric. Sew the new fabric to the unit and press.

Add another fabric.

7. Continue in this manner—cutting, sewing, and pressing—until you have a background that is *at least* 2″ wider and 2″ longer than you need.

8. Press each background block in half vertically and horizontally. Use a pencil to draw a ¼″-long mark over each end of the pressed-in grid lines. Be sure not to make the marks too long or they will show on the block. These little lines make it easier to match up the overlay as you work with it and will help you find the center of the block when needed.

Coping Strips

When sewing blocks or panels together, you may find that one block is a little short. Not to worry—sew some more fabric to it to bring it up to size. These strips are often called "coping strips" because they help you cope when pieces don't fit together.

Coping strip in *Passion Flowers,* page 13

Putting Together the Quilt

Cut the edges of the blocks, sashing, and borders in the same way that you constructed the backgrounds: Place a pressed block right side up on your rotary mat. Place the adjacent sashing or border strip over (or under) the edge of the block. Overlap these edges as necessary. Cut through both fabrics. Discard the excess fabric. Sew and press. Use coping strips as necessary.

As your quilt grows, you will be overlapping and cutting ever-larger units. It helps to do this on a large table. If you have more than one rotary cutting mat, push the mats together under your fabric so you can make long cuts without moving your mat.

If you have constructed your entire quilt without using a ruler, consider trimming the outer edges of your quilt by eye as well. A straight outer edge can look harsh next to the fluid lines in the quilt's interior. You can fold your quilt in half in each direction to see how square (or unsquare) it is before you begin trimming.

Finishing the Quilt

1. Assemble the quilt top, following the instructions for each project.

2. Construct the back of the quilt, piecing as needed.

3. Place the backing right side down on a firm surface. Tape it down to keep it from moving around while you baste.

4. Place the batting over the backing, and *pat* out any wrinkles.

5. Center the quilt top right side up over the batting.

6. Baste the layers together. (Yes, we thread baste for both hand and machine quilting.)

7. Quilt by machine or by hand.

8. Trim the outer edges. Leave ¼″–⅜″ of backing and batting extending beyond the edge of the quilt top. This extra fabric and batting will fill the binding nicely.

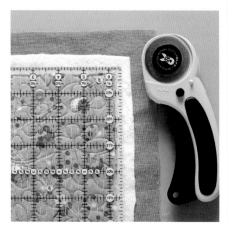

Trim backing and batting.

9. Finish the outer edges with continuous bias binding (refer to Sewing Binding to the Quilt on page 50).

Making Continuous Bias Strips

We use binding cut on the bias grain of the fabric because it wears better. Bias strips also make very good vines, because they are flexible and curve gracefully. We normally cut our binding strips 2½″ wide for binding and 1¾″ to 2″ wide for stems.

BIAS FROM STRIPS

When you want to make a bias strip from more than one fabric, it is easiest to make it by cutting and piecing strips.

1. Cut several strips on the bias at the designated width. Angle both ends at the same 45° angle.

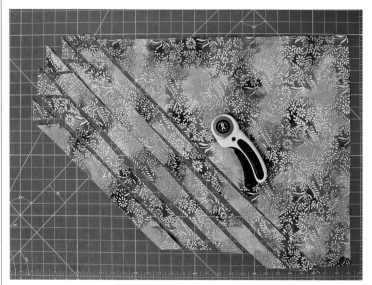

Cut strips on bias with angled ends.

2. Place 2 strips right sides together. Offset the ends so that a V is formed at the ¼″ seamline.

Place strips together with offsetting ends.

3. Sew the strips together end-to-end with a ¼″ seam. Press the seam allowances open.

BIAS FROM A SQUARE

When you need a length of bias made from one fabric, this method works very well. A surprisingly small amount of fabric makes quite a bit of bias, and there is no waste. We show you how to master those tricky binding corners on page 50.

1. Cut a square of fabric in half diagonally. Refer to the project instructions for the size of the square.

2. Sew together the 2 triangles, right sides together, as shown. Be sure to sew the edges that are on the straight of grain. If you are using striped fabric, match the stripes. You may need to offset the fabric a little to make the stripes match.

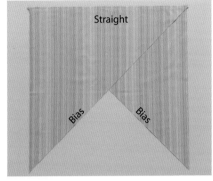

Sew together straight-of-grain edges of triangles.

3. Press the seam allowances open. Make a short cut 2½" in from each side as shown. Cuts are always made on the bias grain of the fabric—check the grain line before you cut.

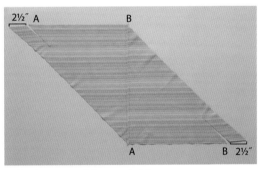

Make short cut 2½" from each side.

4. Match the A's and B's with the fabric right sides together. Pin and sew. Press the seam open.

Pin, sew, and press.

5. Use a rotary cutter and ruler to cut the continuous bias strip 2½" wide, cutting through one layer of the fabric only.

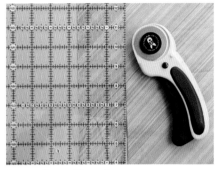

Cut continuous bias strip.

6. For double-fold binding, press together the length of bias strip with wrong sides together.

Continuous Bias Cutting Tip

Try putting a small cutting mat on the end of the ironing board. Slide the tube of fabric over the mat. Use a ruler and rotary cutter to cut a long strip of continuous bias, rotating the tube of fabric as needed. Cut using gentle pressure—if the ironing board is padded, the cutting surface may give if you press too hard.

Sewing Binding to the Quilt

1. Trim the outer edges of the quilt sandwich (refer to Finishing the Quilt on page 48).

2. Cut the first end of the binding at a 45° angle. Turn under this end ½" and press.

3. Press the continuous binding strip in half lengthwise, wrong sides together.

4. With raw edges even, pin the binding to the edge of the quilt, beginning a few inches from a corner. Start sewing 6" from the beginning of the binding strip using a ¼" seam allowance and the walking foot.

Start 6" from beginning of binding; use ¼" seam.

5. Stop ¼" from the corner, and back-stitch several stitches.

6. Fold the binding straight up as shown. Note the 45° angle.

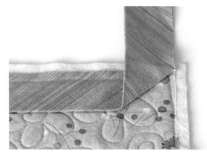

Stop ¼" from corner.

7. Fold the binding straight down, and begin sewing the next side of the quilt.

8. Sew the binding to all sides of the quilt, following the process in Steps 4–7. Stop a few inches before you reach the beginning of the binding, but don't trim the excess binding yet.

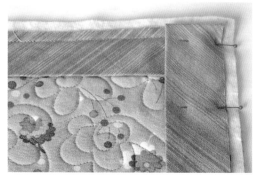

Fold down binding and sew.

9. Overlap the ends of the binding, and cut the second end at a 90° angle. *Be sure to cut the binding long enough so the cut end is covered completely by the angled end.*

10. Turn under ¼", and finger-press the angled end. Slip the 90° end into the angled end.

Slip 90° end into angled end.

11. Pin the joined ends to the quilt, and finish sewing the binding to the quilt.

Pin joined ends, and finish sewing.

12. Turn the binding to the back of the quilt, covering the raw edges. If there is too much batting, trim some to leave your binding nicely filled. Hand stitch the folded edge of the binding to the back of the quilt. Hand stitch the mitered corner edges down.

Making a Label and Sleeve

1. Make a hanging sleeve, and attach it to the back of the quilt.

2. Make a label, and sew it to the back of the quilt. Include information you want people to know about the quilt. Your name and address, the date, the fiber content of the quilt and batting, the special person or occasion the quilt was made for—these are all things that can go on the label.

Signing Your Quilt

We have come to the conclusion that it's a good idea to put your name on the front of your quilt as well putting a label on the back. There are a variety of ways to do this.

You can appliqué your initials and the date on the quilt top. You can add information with embroidery or a permanent pen. Or you can quilt your name and the date into your quilt with matching or contrasting thread.

General Appliqué Instructions

Making the Appliqué Templates

Each appliqué shape requires a template, and we have a unique way of making templates that is both easy and accurate.

1. Use a photocopier to make 2–3 copies of each block. If the pattern needs to be enlarged or reduced, make these changes *before* making copies. Always compare the copies with the original to be sure they are accurate.

Determining the Number of Copies

You need a complete paper shape for each appliqué piece that requires a template. When one shape lies over another, you need two copies. Look at each shape to determine how many copies it requires— or make three copies of each pattern, knowing that you'll probably have some extra copies.

2. Cut out the appliqué shapes from these copies. Cut them in groups when possible, as this saves on the laminate (refer to Basic Supplies on page 6). Leave a little paper allowance around each shape or group. Where one shape overlaps another, cut the top shape from one copy and the bottom shape from another copy.

3. Place a self-laminating sheet shiny side down on the table. Peel off the paper backing, leaving the sticky side of the sheet facing up.

4. For **hand appliqué,** place the templates *drawn* side down on the self-laminating sheet. For **fusible appliqué,** place the templates *blank* side down. Take care when placing each template onto the laminate. Use more laminating sheets as necessary.

For hand appliqué, place appliqué shapes *drawn* side down on self-laminating sheets.

For fusible appliqué, place appliqué shapes *blank* side down on self-laminating sheets.

5. Cut out each shape. Try to split the drawn line with your scissors—don't cut inside or outside the line. Keep edges smooth and points sharp.

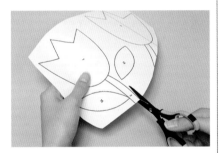

Cut out each template.

You'll notice how easy these templates are to cut out. That's the main reason we like this method. It is also true that a mechanical copy of the pattern is more accurate than hand tracing onto template plastic. As you use the templates, you will see that they are sturdy and hold up to repeated use.

Making Big Templates

Many of the appliqué shapes are big—bigger than a sheet of paper. When this is the case, make a big copy, if possible. Copiers that make very large copies are becoming much more common. Be sure to check with your local copy services to see if they can enlarge these patterns in one step onto large paper. Otherwise copy the shape onto as many sheets of paper as necessary, and overlap and tape the copies together to make the whole shape. Place the shape on laminate as described at left. Overlap pieces of laminate as necessary to fit the whole shape.

Using the Templates

The numbers on the templates indicate the stitching sequence. Begin with 1, and work your way through the block. The templates are used with the shiny laminate side up. **Hand appliqué** templates are placed on the right side of the fabric with the drawn shiny side up. **Fusible appliqué** templates are placed on the wrong side of the fabric with the blank shiny side up.

>
> **tip**
>
> We have reservations about recommending fusible web. We aren't sure how the chemicals in it will affect fabric over time. However, if you choose to use fusible web, follow the manufacturer's instructions. Use a nonstick pressing cloth to protect the iron and ironing board from the fusible web. Be sure to test the fabrics you plan to use. Iron the fusible web to the *wrong* side of the appliqué fabric. Do not peel off the paper backing until later.

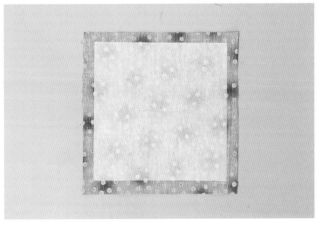

Iron fusible web to *wrong* side of fabric.

1. For **hand appliqué,** place the appliqué fabric right side up on a sandpaper board (refer to Basic Supplies on page 6). For **fusible appliqué,** place the fabric with the wrong side up. (The fusible web side will be up.)

2. Place the template right side up (shiny laminate side up) on the fabric, with as many edges as possible on the diagonal grain of the fabric. A bias edge is easier to turn under (hand appliqué) and will fray less than one on the straight of grain.

3. Trace around the template. The sandpaper board will hold the fabric in place while you trace. Make a line you can see. Be sure to draw the line right next to the edge of the template. It won't matter if the line is wide. It gets turned under in hand appliqué. For fusible appliqué, trace on the paper with the template wrong side up.

Trace template onto fabric for hand appliqué.

Trace template onto paper backing for fusible appliqué.

Place templates with as many edges as possible on bias.

Using Templates Loosely

When working loosely or improvisationally, trace around the template—sort of. Draw the shape bigger or smaller. Make it longer or shorter. You may alter all or only some of the appliqué shapes in a pattern.

Change shape of appliqué piece.

4. For **hand appliqué,** cut out each appliqué piece, adding a ³⁄₁₆″ turn-under allowance. Add a scant ³⁄₈″ allowance to any part of an appliqué piece that lies under another piece.

For **fusible appliqué,** cut out each appliqué piece on the drawn line. Add a scant ¹⁄₁₆″ allowance to any part of an appliqué piece that lies under another piece. Do not remove the paper backing from the fusible appliqué pieces until you are ready to position each piece on the block.

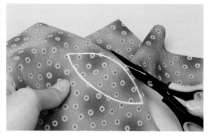

Hand appliqué   Fusible appliqué

Cut out each appliqué piece.

Making the Positioning Overlay

The positioning overlay is a piece of clear vinyl (refer to Basic Supplies on page 6) that is used to accurately position each appliqué piece on the block. The overlay is easy to make and use, and it makes your projects portable. It can be used with just about any appliqué method.

1. Cut a piece of the vinyl to the finished size of each block. (If your vinyl has a tissue paper lining, cut the vinyl and tissue at the same time, and set aside the tissue paper until you are ready to fold or store the overlay.)

2. Enlarge the patterns in this book as necessary. Tape pattern pieces together as needed.

Making Big Copies

Copiers that make very large copies are becoming much more common. Be sure to check with your local copy services to see if they can enlarge these patterns in one step onto large paper.

3. Tape the pattern onto a table.

4. Tape the vinyl over the pattern. Use a ruler and a fine-point permanent marker (refer to Basic Supplies on page 6) to draw the pattern's horizontal and vertical center lines onto the vinyl.

Tape vinyl over pattern, and draw center lines.

5. Accurately trace all the lines from the pattern onto the vinyl. The numbers on the pattern indicate the stitching sequence—include these numbers on the overlay. These numbers also tell you which side of the overlay is the right side.

6. Draw a small X in one corner of the positioning overlay.

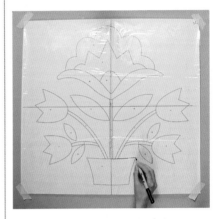

Trace pattern onto vinyl. Draw small X in one corner of overlay.

7. To store the overlay, place the tissue paper over the drawn side of the overlay, and fold or roll them together.

Using the Positioning Overlay

Refer to Using Positioning Overlays Loosely (page 57) before using your overlay.

1. Place the background fabric right side up on the work surface. For **hand appliqué,** work on top of the sandpaper board, as the sandpaper keeps the background from shifting as you position appliqué pieces on the block. For **fusible appliqué,** work on your ironing surface.

2. Place the overlay right side up on top of the background, lining up the pressed-in center lines on your background with the center lines of the overlay.

> The first time you use the overlay for a block, mark an X on the block in the same corner as on the overlay so that you always know how to position the overlay.

3. If necessary, pin the overlay to keep it from shifting out of position. Flat flower-head pins work best.

Place overlay on background, and line up center lines.

4. For **hand appliqué,** finger-press the turn-under allowances before placing the appliqué pieces on the block. This is a *very important step* for hand appliqué. As you finger-press, make sure that the drawn line is pressed to the back. This one step makes needle-turning the turn-under allowance much easier.

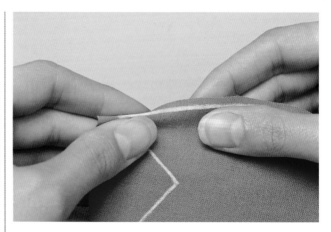

Finger-press each piece with drawn line to back.

Finger-Pressing

It bears repeating—finger-pressing is a very important step in needle-turn hand appliqué. You'll be amazed at how much easier this one step makes needle-turning the turn-under allowance.

Hold the appliqué piece right side up. Use your thumb and index finger to turn the turn-under allowance to the back of the appliqué so the chalk line is just barely turned under. If you can see the chalk line on the top of your appliqué, it will be visible after it is sewn.

Use your fingers to press a crease into the fabric along the inside of the chalk line. Good-quality 100% cotton will hold a finger-press very well. Do not wet your fingers, do not use starch, and do not scrape your fingernail along the crease. Just pinch it with your fingertips. Finger-press every edge that will be sewn down.

Appliqué pieces that are cut freehand will not have a chalk line to turn under. In this case, turn under a 3⁄16″ turn-under allowance by eye. As you are sewing, the fabric will turn on the crease.

5. For **fusible appliqué,** remove the paper backing from each appliqué piece as you go. Be careful not to stretch or ravel the outer edges.

6. Place the appliqué pieces right side up under the overlay but on top of the background. This makes it easy to tell when the appliqué pieces are in position under the overlay. Start with appliqué piece 1, and follow the appliqué order. For **hand appliqué,** finger-press and position one piece at a time. For **fusible appliqué,** you may be able to position several pieces at once, but don't position too many at a time.

Hand appliqué

Fusible appliqué

Use overlay to position appliqué pieces.

7. For **hand appliqué,** fold back the overlay, and pin the appliqué pieces in place. You can pin against the sandpaper board—doing so will not dull the pins. We usually position and stitch only 1 or 2 pieces at a time. Remove the vinyl overlay before

stitching. Use ½″ sequin pins, placing pins parallel to the chalk line and ¼″ inside the line. It is often easier to baste large pieces to your background. If you baste, baste securely parallel to the chalk line, ¼″ inside the line.

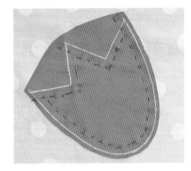

Pin appliqué piece in place.

Baste large appliqué pieces in place.

8. For **hand appliqué,** sew the pieces in place with an invisible stitch and matching thread. For **fusible appliqué,** carefully remove the overlay, and iron the appliqué pieces in place, following the fusible web manufacturer's instructions. Do not touch the overlay vinyl with the iron because the vinyl will melt.

9. We recommend that if you fuse, you stitch the edges of the fused pieces by hand or on the sewing machine. A blanket stitch in matching thread will lend a more traditional feel to the fabrics. As the quilts are used, the stitching also keeps the edges secure.

10. When you are ready to put away the overlay, place the saved tissue paper over the drawn side before you fold it. The tissue paper keeps the lines from transferring from one part of the vinyl to another.

Using Positioning Overlays Loosely

Use the overlay to position the primary stems on the background, but feel free to tilt or move a piece if you want to—just keep in mind that you may need to adjust the placement of other pieces so the block looks balanced. Position the majority of the remaining appliqué pieces by eye. If this makes you nervous, use the overlay to position appliqué pieces, but don't be particularly precise.

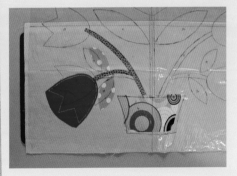

Place appliqué pieces less precisely.

Positioning Appliqué Shapes on the Design Wall

Refer to Design Wall (page 11).

Some quilts do not require a pattern. *Picasso's Garden* (page 27), for example, has very simple appliqué shapes that are cut by hand and placed by eye.

Construct the backgrounds as directed, and place them on the design wall. Cut the appliqué shapes, and place them on the backgrounds on the design wall until you have everything just the way you want it.

The real trick when you are working without a pattern is maintaining the position of the appliqué pieces just as you have them on the wall. You have two options for doing this.

Positioning Option 1

Cut vinyl to the size of the backgrounds for positioning overlays. On the design wall, pin the vinyl over the appliqué and background. Trace the appliqué shapes with an ultra-fine-point marker. This is a tedious method.

Positioning Option 2

Use ½" sequin pins to pin the appliqué shapes through the backgrounds into the design wall. Stick the pins straight into the design wall (don't use longer pins, as they get in the way). When all the appliqué pieces are pinned, grab the bottom corners of the background, and *gently* pull the background off the wall. The pins will keep the appliqué pieces in place.

Place the background (pins and all) right side up on a table. Baste the appliqué shapes in place, removing the pins as you go. It is a good idea to baste well. Keep your basting stitches relatively short, and place them where you would normally place your appliqué pins. Handle the block carefully to keep fraying to a minimum.

Pressing and Trimming the Blocks

After the appliqué is complete, press the blocks on the wrong side. If the ironing surface is hard, place the blocks on a towel so the appliqué will not get flattened. Be careful not to stretch the blocks as you press.

Take your time when trimming your blocks to size. Be sure of your measurements *before* you cut. If you are using a ruler, remember to measure twice, and cut once. If you are working improvisationally, use the grid on your cutting mat to trim your blocks to the approximate size.

1. Press the blocks on the wrong side.

2. Carefully trim each block to size. When using a ruler, measure from the center out. Regardless of how you measure (or not), always make sure the design is properly aligned before you cut off the excess fabric.

Visible Appliqué Stitches

Invisible appliqué stitches are *invisible* and are therefore not really part of the design. Occasionally, a design will benefit from some very *visible* appliqué stitches.

Many of the leaves in *Leaves in the Breeze* (page 21) have appliqué stitches that are almost like embroidery. Needle-turn the edge under, and stitch it down using any stitch that does the job. Becky chose to use cotton hand quilting thread for its thickness and durability.

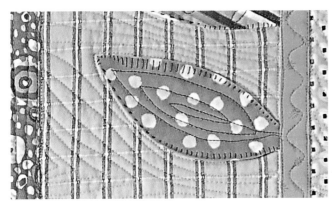

Be creative! Think of stitches as embellishments.

Cutaway Appliqué

The cutaway technique makes it much easier to stitch irregular, long, thin, or very small pieces. It is especially good to use for narrow stems or the curlicues in *Tree O' Life* (page 34).

1. Place the template on top of the selected fabric. Be sure to place the template on the fabric so that most of the edges will be on the diagonal grain of the fabric. Trace around the template (be as precise or as loose as you like).

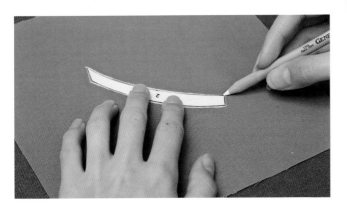

Place template with as many edges as possible on bias, and trace around template.

Special Techniques

2. Cut out the appliqué piece, leaving 1″ or more of excess fabric around the traced shape. Leave fabric intact in the V between points, inside deep curves, and so on.

3. Finger-press, making sure the drawn line is pressed to the back. Don't worry about the excess fabric; you will cut it off as you sew.

4. Use the vinyl positioning overlay to position the appliqué piece on the block.

5. If your piece is not basted, place pins ¼″ from the finger-pressed edge. Place pins parallel to the edges. Large pieces, such as the basket handles, can be basted in place if you prefer. First pin the shape in place; then baste it. When a shape is curved, sew the concave side first, if possible. When shapes are narrow, one row of pins may be sufficient. In this case, place pins ¼″ from the edge that you will sew first.

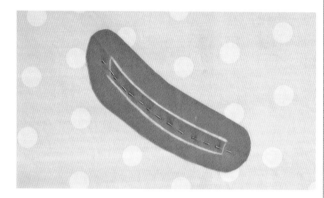

Pin appliqué piece in place. Baste large shapes.

6. Begin cutting away the excess fabric from where you will start stitching, leaving a ³⁄₁₆″ turn-under allowance. Never start stitching at an inner or outer point that will be turned under.

Cut away excess fabric, and begin stitching.

7. Trim more fabric as you sew. Clip inner curves and inner points as needed.

8. Remove the pins as you stitch the next edge of the piece. Trim excess fabric as necessary.

9. Continue until all edges of the appliqué piece are stitched.

Circle Appliqué

When sewing outer curves and circles, you can only control one stitch at a time. Use the needle or a round wooden toothpick to smooth out any pleats that form. Remember, the more you practice, the better you'll get.

1. Prepare and position the circles as you would any other appliqué piece. Cut out circles with a *scant* ³⁄₁₆″ turn-under allowance. Finger-press each circle. If you are pinning rather than basting, use at least 2 pins to keep the circle from shifting.

2. Begin sewing. Turn under only enough turn-under allowance to take 1 or 2 stitches. If you turn under more, the appliquéd curve will have flat spaces and points.

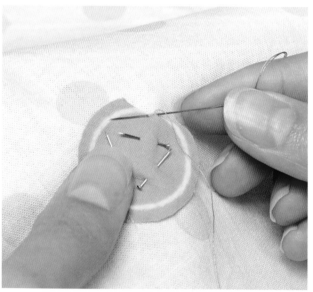

Turn under only enough for 1 or 2 stitches.

3. Use the tip of the needle or a toothpick to reach under the appliqué to spread open any folds and to smooth out any points.

As seen from back: Use needle to open folds and to smooth points.

4. To close the circle, turn under the last few stitches all at once. The circle will tend to flatten out.

5. Use the tip of the needle to smooth out the pleats in the turn-under allowance and to pull the flattened part of the circle into a more rounded shape.

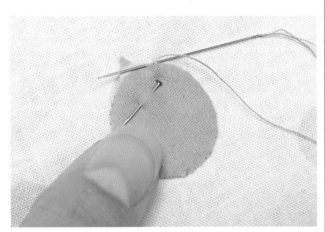

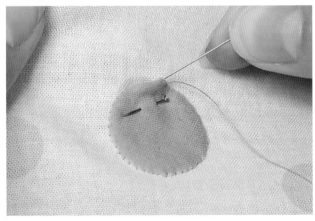

Finish stitching circle.

Organic Bias Stems

The long stems and vines in these quilts are not uniform in width. This gives them an organic quality that works well with the looser placement and expressive pieced lines. This means you shouldn't use bias bars to make the stems in this book, because those bars make stems too uniform in width.

1. Without using a ruler, cut bias strips roughly ⅞″ wide. Your strip width will vary, and that's okay.

2. Sew the strips together end-to-end (refer to Bias from Strips on page 48).

3. Baste the long bias strip to the background. One line of basting stitches down the center is probably sufficient. Finger-press the edges under as you go, and sew the bias stem to the background.

Bias vine from *Picasso's Garden* (page 27)

About the Authors

The Green Country Quilters Guild in Tulsa, Oklahoma, can be credited with bringing together Linda Jenkins and Becky Goldsmith. Their friendship developed while they worked together on many guild projects and through their shared love for appliqué. This partnership led to the birth of Piece O' Cake Designs in 1994 and has survived a variety of moves. Currently, Linda lives in Grand Junction, Colorado, and Becky lives in Sherman, Texas.

Linda owned and managed a beauty salon before she started quilting. Over the years, she developed a fine eye for color as a hair colorist and makeup artist. Becky's degree in interior design and her many art classes provided a perfect background for quilting. Linda and Becky have shown many quilts and have won numerous awards. Together, they make a dynamic quilting duo and love to teach other quilters the joys of appliqué—and piecing!

In the fall of 2002, Becky and Linda joined the C&T Publishing family, where they continue to produce wonderful books and patterns.

Visit the Piece O' Cake Designs website at www.pieceocake.com.

Also by Becky Goldsmith and Linda Jenkins:

Index

Useful Information

Projects

**For appliqué supplies, including
Karen Buckley Perfect Circles:**

www.pieceocake.com

Great Titles *from* C&T PUBLISHING

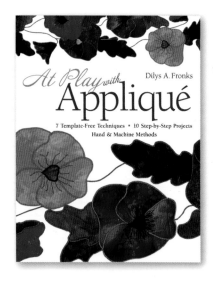

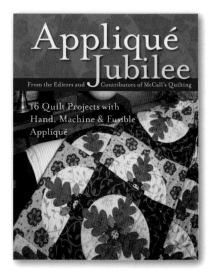

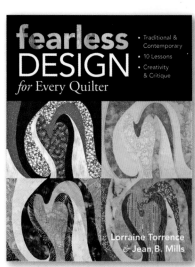

Available at your local retailer or **www.ctpub.com** or **800.284.1114**

For a list of other fine books from C&T Publishing,
ask for a free catalog:

C&T PUBLISHING, INC.

P.O. Box 1456

Lafayette, CA 94549

(800) 284-1114

Email: ctinfo@ctpub.com

Website: www.ctpub.com

C&T Publishing's professional photography services are now available
to the public. Visit us at www.ctmediaservices.com.

For quilting supplies:

COTTON PATCH

1025 Brown Ave.

Lafayette, CA 94549

Store: (925) 284-1177

Mail order: (925) 283-7883

Email: CottonPa@aol.com

Website: www.quiltusa.com

Note: Fabrics used in the quilts shown may not be currently
available, as fabric manufacturers keep most fabrics in
print for only a short time.